The Water People

Gens de l'eau

'This beautifully readable, book-length sequence combines epic and lyric, history and song, magic and realism. The water people are not spirits or naiads, confined to mysterious pools or vague archetype. Sturdy and resourceful, profoundly at home among their forests and stony hills, they are essentially human, and might even be our ancestors ... River-fresh and supple in Marilyn Hacker's English translation, Khoury-Ghata's voice has the authority and cadence of the practised story-teller. While morally alert, she avoids message-preaching, dodges abstraction. Symbols are never merely symbolic but tangible objects, weighed in the hands, felt under the feet ... The re-telling of traditional stories and fables is an enduringly popular genre in contemporary poetry. Vénus Khoury-Ghata has gone farther, inventing a new 'ancient' mythology which has a particular relevance to the present moment. Her water people mirror our own potential, and challenge the violence and materialism of the post-20th century. Their parables show us how we might recover our natural humanity, and live in harmony with ourselves, our fellow-earth people – and our earth.'

Carol Rumens

Vénus Khoury-Ghata

The Water People
Gens de l'eau

Translated from French by
Marilyn Hacker

poetry
translation
centre

First published in 2022
by the Poetry Translation Centre Ltd
The Albany, Douglas Way, London, SE8 4AG

www.poetrytranslation.org

ISBN: 978-1-7398948-0-1

A catalogue record for this book is available from the British Library

Typeset in Minion by Poetry Translation Centre Ltd

Series Editor: Nashwa Gowanlock
Cover Design: Kit Humphrey
Printed in the UK by T J Books Limited

This publication has been supported by the European Union's Creative
Europe culture programme which funds literary translations.

The Poetry Translation Centre is supported using public funding by Arts
Council England.

Contents

Introduction

Vénus Khoury-Ghata was born in Bcharré, a village in northern Lebanon, also the birthplace of Gibran Khalil Gibran. Raised in Beirut, she was not a child of the intelligentsia or the diplomatic world like many literary émigrés. She was born to a Maronite Christian family, one of four children of a bilingual policeman and a housewife she has described as 'illiterate in two languages'. Her one brother, an aspiring poet, was interned in a mental hospital, where he died. One of her sisters, May Menassa, who stayed in Lebanon, became a journalist and fiction writer. Vénus, who has lived in France since 1972, and her second husband, the Armenian physician Jean Ghata, became part of – indeed created – a polycultural and polyglot literary scene, where writers of French, Lebanese, Canadian, Swedish, Kurdish backgrounds gathered in their sitting-room over coffee, or even a long lunch of home-prepared Lebanese mezze.

Although her mother tongue (and her mother's tongue) is Arabic, Khoury-Ghata has become a major figure in what was until recently – when this idea began to seem somewhat imperialist – labelled as Francophone writing, the literature of those who, as the Algerian playwright and poet Kateb Yacine stated, 'write in French to tell the French that I am not French'. Writers from the Middle East, the Maghreb, sub-Saharan Africa, the West Indies, Canada and Belgium, who live in their own countries or in France and who write in French, have enriched and renewed the energy of French poetry and fiction for more than a century. One of the things they continue to bring is a poetry rich in narrative specificity, fantasy, satire and political engagement that goes against the grain of a post-Mallarméan abstraction.

A prolific writer across genres, Vénus Khoury-Ghata is now the author of 23 novels and 21 collections of poems. Soon after settling in France, she made a conscious choice of French as her language of expression. Like many Lebanese children of all social classes, French was the language of her schooling, and her officer father's preferred language, while Arabic was literally her unlettered mother's tongue. Vénus herself has in the last decades translated contemporary poetry from Arabic, including several recent collections by the Syrian-Lebanese poet Adonis, known as a major transformative figure in Arabic modernism. The Arabic language, as she herself states, often seems to speak through her French in the elaborate, pithy figurative language in which she delights, in the landscapes and seasons through which her poems' protagonists (hers are poems with protagonists) move – and it's a Lebanese Arabic, with its own history, its music, its proverbs.

Though Vénus has lived in Paris for decades, the implied landscape of her densely populated poems (unlike her novels and non-fiction) is always Lebanese, in fluid transformation from a fable-textured place of origin to the warscape of yesterday's news. She writes: 'Nourished by the two languages, I write in Arabic through the French language – when my poems are translated into Arabic, they seem to be returning to their original language. For years, my first drafts were written in both languages, the Arabic going from right to left on the page and the French from left to right: they crossed each other's paths in the middle. Three decades in Paris haven't cured me of my mother tongue!'

Vénus's poems, composed for the most part in sequences, often have the quality of exploded narratives, reassembled in a mosaic in which the reader has at least the illusion of being able to find a connecting thread. The same themes which animate her fiction are predominant in the poems: the tension between movement/change and tradition/sources, with all that is positive and negative in both; the unceasing commerce

8

between human beings and the rest of the natural world, and between the dead and the living; the independent, puissant and transcultural life of languages and of words.

The Water People (*Gens de l'eau*) was published in Paris in 2018, a semi-surreal sequence set in one of the poet's populous dreamscapes, which resembles nothing as much as a village in the mountains of Lebanon, with a river and its mini-waterfall close by, and Beirut as distant as Beijing, akin to – but more mysterious than – the folk-tale sequences featuring a named carpenter, midwife, priest, teacher. The men are hunters, not farmers or shopkeepers. There is a shamaness, but not a schoolteacher or a priest. There is no church or mosque, and no school, though there are many children. The people interact with the elements, with plants and animals – a wolf figures largely, but so do trees – as they do with each other. Trees, stones, and of course rivers, streams, waterfalls, have as much identity, and individuality, as the woman – one of many, it seems, crouched over her pots and pans. Or the man who seems to have died, maybe to be reborn, in the forest. Yet all these folk-tale figures are also avatars of the poet's history – her own mother's mountain village, Bcharré, the beloved physician husband, Jean Ghata, who died young, the third husband who died old, the children and grandchildren scattered across two continents, and the war that scythed across the poet's youth.

Reading *The Water People* is at once immersion in an intriguing folk-tale, and discovery (or rediscovery) of a unique voice in French poetry, with its own pervasive music, that insists on the importance and the possibilities of narrative in lyric poems.

Marilyn Hacker

Poems

Gens de l'eau [extraits]

Pleure comme si la rivière était entrée en toi
disent les gens de l'eau
Et laisse ta voix derrière toi pour mieux t'écouter par temps de pluie

les gens de l'eau ont leurs codes pris au premier saule
ils parlent la bouche remplie d'abeilles
le caillou blanc sur la langue signe la paix

les gens de l'eau dans leur vieille vieillesse
se laissent escalader par les jeunes pousses
le chemin partira sans eux
leur feu grandira seul

assis sur la cendre des braises
les vieux de vieillesse soufflent sur les nuages étrangers
ceux qui retombent sur leurs pieds appelés brouillard
    bienveillant

from *The Water People*

Weep as if the river had entered you
say the water people
And leave your voice behind to listen better when it rains

the water people took their codes from the first willow
they speak with their mouths full of bees
a white pebble on the tongue as a sign of peace

in their oldest old age the water people
let young tendrils and buds climb over them
the road will leave without them
and their fire grow by itself

sitting on the glowing embers
the oldest of the old blow on the foreign clouds
those that land on their feet are called benevolent fog

Un sac de rires pour le garçon qui porte une coccinelle sur
    l'épaule
une calebasse à quatre noeuds pour celle qui arrache un ruisseau
    à la terre pour laver le sang menstruel du grenadier

les femmes des gens de l'eau dessinent leur visage de nuit avec la
    suie de leur marmite
trèfle à quatre feuilles leur empreinte sur les reins de l'homme
    qui dort à plat ventre sur sa fatigue

***

Un lance-pierre en jonc pour l'enfant né entre chien et loup
une herbe rouge sur la paume de la fille pubère
sa mère lui apprendra à épiler les arbres femelles et plumer la
    volaille vivante

y a-t-il d'autres mères de l'autre côté de l'horizon se
    demandent les mères à chaque crépuscule
essorent-elles leurs murs après la pluie
leur feu transi fait-il bouillir leur marmite

***

A bag of laughter for the boy with a ladybird on his
    shoulder
a four-knotted calabash for the girl who uproots a stream
    from the earth to wash off the pomegranate tree's
    menstrual blood

the women of the water people draw their night-time faces
    with the soot of their casseroles
their handprint a four-leaf clover on the small of the back of
    the man sleeping belly-down on his own exhaustion

***

A bulrush slingshot for the child born at twilight
a blade of red grass on the pubescent girl's palm
her mother will teach her to shave the female trees' armpits
    and pluck the chickens while they're still alive

are there other mothers beyond the horizon the mothers ask
    themselves each day at dusk
do they wring out the walls after the rain
does their bone-chilled fire make their pots boil?

***

Peau de zébu et linge humide sèchent côte à côte
sera pendu à la corde de sa mère celui qui a percé la fille verte
    et l'écorce du jeune bouleau

un chevreau de l'année pour l'homme qui a enjambé la colline
    sans faire sursauter les cailloux

dépecé à mains nues
ses os nourriront ceux qui mangent avec leurs orteils
front entre les genoux
ainsi

***

Les femmes des gens de l'eau donnent à manger dans leur
    main au tigre
mais chassent à coups de bâton la fourmi sous l'oreiller

les nuages qui pleurent par beau temps est leur ombre
    inversée
leur noir arc-en-ciel
c'est lui qui marie la huppe avec le lézard
l'ange avec la mésange
lui qui s'affale sur leur seuil au coup de feu du chasseur
avec un accroc au cœur

***

Antelope pelt and wet laundry dry side by side
they'll be hung out on her mother's line, that went through
    the green girl and the young birch tree's bark

a yearling kid for the man who strode over the hill without
    startling the pebbles

dismembered bare-handed
its bones will feed those who eat with their toes
forehead between their knees
like this

***

The women of the water people feed the tiger with their bare
    hands
but they chase an ant from under the pillow with a stick

the clouds that weep in fine weather are their shadow turned
    inside out
their black rainbow
who marries the hoopoe to the lizard
the angel to the blue jay
who collapses in their doorway when the hunter fires his gun
with a heart torn open

***

à Bernard Pivot

Faute de miroir
les femmes des gens de l'eau ne savent pas qu'elles sont
    femmes
l'herbe arrachée de la main gauche
les imprègne de sa soumission
elles tissent des murs autour de leurs hanches quand l'homme
    part à la chasse
coupent le fil à son retour avec leurs dents
l'antilope sur l'épaule n'est pas un gibier
mais une épouse pour temps d'indigence et de désillusions

***

à Diane de Bournazel

Armé de sa rage
l'homme chasse pour entendre ses déflagrations trouer le ciel
pour faire pleuvoir et donner à boire à son plant de maïs

assieds-toi sur ce caillou et observe les semelles du jujubier lui
    dit sa femme
elles ne doivent rien au forgeron

***

for Bernard Pivot

For want of a mirror
the women of the water people don't know that they are
    women
grass uprooted left-handed
imbues them with submission
they weave walls around their hips when the men go off
    hunting
cut the thread with their teeth when they return
an antelope over the shoulder isn't game
but a spouse for seasons of poverty and disillusion

***

for Diane de Bournazel

Armed with his anger
the man hunts to hear his explosions pierce the sky
to make it rain and quench his corn stalks' thirst

sit down on this pebble and watch the soles of the jujube tree,
    says his wife
the blacksmith couldn't do better

inusables les sabots de ceux qui marchent sous terre sans se
    déplacer
pas de chaussures qui traînent derrière soi lorsqu'on décide de
    mourir
mais l'écho d'une voix qui lézarde les murs

***

Les femmes des gens de l'eau donnent le pain d'orge au cheval
les graines du canari à l'homme qui a ouvert la cage
puis l'enterrent au pied de l'if
qu'il meure si telle est la volonté de l'oiseau parti sans réfléchir
la veuve sait comment l'assouplir pour l'introduire dans la
    terre sans casser ses os

les gens de l'eau enterrent leurs morts derrière la cascade
leurs appels transmis par l'eau criarde
ils ne doivent rien à personne

seule l'eau qui marche à grandes enjambées sait laver les
    souffrances disent-ils

the clogs of those who walk under the earth without moving
    never wear out
no shoes trail behind you when you decide to die
just the echo of a voice that cracks the walls

***

The women of the water people give barley bread to the horse
grains of bird food to the man who opened the cage
then bury him at the foot of the yew tree
let him die if that's the wish of the bird who flew off unreflecting
the widow knows how to make him more supple to slip him
    into the earth without breaking his bones

the water people bury their dead behind the waterfall
their voices are carried by the noisy water
they owe nothing to anyone

only the water that strides along knows how to wash away
    suffering, they say

***

Consulter l'arbre de l'empathie ne sert qu'aux morts disent-ils
    là-haut
le vol des vautours lu à l'envers annonce consolation et
    prospérité
l'homme riche de sept bêches enterrera dans le même trou
    son vieux cheval et sa récolte pourrie
marcher sur la crête de la colline lui vaut l'estime du loup
leurs empoignades sont fraternelles
peaux sueurs halètements
les connaissances laissées à ceux de la plaine
faute de livre ils lisent l'intérieur des pierres

les gens de l'eau interprètent à leur convenance les paroles
    cueillies sur les lèvres de l'étranger
leur surdité les protège des désillusions

***

La femme des gens de l'eau grave le visage de son défunt
    sur l'envers de la pierre pour le protéger des herbes
    voraces

la mort plus longue au début
elle allume sa lanterne en plein jour
fait crier le silence sous son balai

***

Asking advice of the empathy tree is only good for the dead,
    they say up there
vultures' flight read backwards announces consolation and
    prosperity
the man whose wealth is seven spades will bury his old horse
    and his decaying harvest in the same hole
walking on the hill ridge earns him the wolf's esteem
their arguments are fraternal
skin sweat panting
their knowledge left to the plains-dwellers
for lack of a book they read the insides of stones

the water people interpret as they please the words gathered
    from the stranger's lips
their deafness protects them from disappointment

***

The woman of the water people engraves the face of her
    dead man on the underside of a stone to protect it from
    voracious grasses

death is longest at the beginning
she lights her lantern in the middle of the day
makes silence shout under her broom

fait plier l'échine à la mort
la met à genoux

son feu attaché à sa ceinture
elle traque la nuit voleuse d'apparence
réclame à celui qui sèche entre deux pierres un miroir qui
    refléterait ses traits

***

La femme seule n'allume plus sa lampe pour recompter son
    âge et ses cuillères en bois
le voleur d'âmes tapi sous la cendre est aussi voleur
    d'étincelles
patience du brouillard qui a rampé jusqu'à sa porte pour
    l'entendre invectiver le feu
seule comme les jours impairs
elle donne à boire au feu
à manger au ruisseau qui convoie ses appels à l'homme
    émietté

la tristesse enserre ses chevilles lorsqu'elle entrouvre la terre à
    sa recherche
autant la creuser pour voir si la graine a poussé

makes death submit
go down on its knees

her fire attached to her belt
she hunts down night that seems to be a thief
asks the one who's drying out between two stones for a mirror
    that will reflect his features

***

The woman alone no longer lights a lamp to count her years
    and her wooden spoons
the thief of souls crouching under the ashes is also a thief of
    sparks
patience of the fog that crept up to her door to hear her shout
    at the fire
alone as odd-numbered days
she gives the fire something to drink
something to eat to the stream that conveys her messages to
    the man crumbled to bits

sorrow clasps her ankles as she opens the earth searching for
    him
she might as well dig to see if a seed had sprouted

***

Compter les empreintes du renard sur le sol rouge ne lui
    rendra pas sa poule

laver les plumes tachées de sang occupe ses mains
et gonflera son oreiller aplati par incompréhension et deuil

les femmes des gens de l'eau ont droit à un coq mais à trois
    hommes
nécessaires quand
les terres hibernent
souffler sur les braises éteintes réveille celui mort sans leur
    permission

***

Séparer le jour de la nuit fait tinter les bracelets de la
    parturiente
le pain qui crie sous sa main a la mémoire du premier sang et
    la fente du premier sillon
pain et pierre se mangeaient crus à l'époque
marcher sur le pied du ruisseau faisait monter le niveau d'eau
    de l'océan avait dit la chamane
mais personne ne l'a contredite

***

Counting the fox's paw prints on the red earth won't bring her
hen back

washing the bloodstained feathers occupies her hands
and will puff up her pillow flattened by incomprehension and
mourning

the women of the water people are entitled to one rooster but
to three men
necessary when
the fields hibernate
they blow on the fading embers to wake the one who died
without their permission

***

Separating day from night makes the bracelets of the woman
in labour jangle
the bread that cries out beneath her hand remembers the first
blood and the cleft of the first furrow
at that time bread and stone were eaten raw
if you step on the stream's foot it will make the ocean's
water level rise the shamaness had said
and no one contradicted her

***

La chamane dit :
répète trois fois le mot herse à ton champ et tu cueilleras ton
    maïs sans quitter ton hamac
fais la sourde oreille au crépuscule
les empoignades entre murs et ténèbres ne te regardent pas
leur vacarme fera reculer ta lanterne d'un jour

combien faut-il d'allumettes au soleil pour qu'il lèche les
    sabots du noyer
devenu bossu à force de ramasser ses fruits

***

La femme qui arrache à main nue l'herbe de son champ doit
    tout à l'homme
au grincement de son échelle adossée au mur
au crissement de l'abeille dans son bol ébréché
même au loup qu'il tuait toutes les nuits dans son sommeil

sa corde sur l'épaule
il marchait au bord du ravin
un pied dans le vide
un pied sur le cœur de celle qui le regardait s'éloigner
sûre qu'il reviendra après extinction du dernier loup

***

Said the shamaness:
repeat the word harrow three times to your field and you'll
    harvest the corn without leaving your hammock
turn a deaf ear to the dusk
arguments between walls and shadows are none of your business
their racket will set your lantern back by a day

how many matches will the sun need to lick the feet of the
    walnut tree
that became a hunchback from bending to gather its fruits

***

The woman who pulls up the grass from her field barehanded
    owes everything to the man
to the creaking of his ladder that leans on the wall
to the buzzing of the bee in his chipped bowl
even to the wolf whom he kills every night in his sleep

a rope on his shoulder
he would walk at the edge of the ravine
one foot in the void
one foot on the heart of the one who watched him going away
sure that he would return when the last wolf was destroyed

***

Les femmes des gens de l'eau connaissent beaucoup de mots
    mais pas le livre qu'ils habitent
que font-ils quand les gens dorment
écartent-ils les pages pour crier
et comment s'expliquer avec ceux venus d'un autre alphabet
écrit de gauche à droite dans le sens contraire du cœur

***

Celui qui a troué le nuage avec son lance-pierre n'aura qu'une
    flaque d'eau pour le pleurer
la date de sa mort inscrite dans le livre des livres
sur la ligne qui ramène dans ses chaussures le défunt
    qui paie son tribut à la pluie qui multiplie blé et
    descendance

quand je serai grand je serai blanc dit l'enfant et il frotte son
    visage avec la neige
le réécrit

***

The women of the water people know many words but not
    the book where they live
what do the words do when people are sleeping
do they spread the pages apart to cry out
and how do they communicate with the ones from another
    alphabet
written from left to right in the opposite direction from the heart

***

The man who pierced the cloud with his slingshot will have
    only a puddle to weep for him
the date of his death inscribed in the book of books
on the line that brings the dead man back upright in his
    shoes to pay tribute to the rain that multiplies wheat and
    offspring

when I'm grown up I'll be white says the child and he rubs
    snow on his face
rewrites it

***

Les femmes mortes en couches renaissent en animal à plume
leur duvet garnit les oreillers
le clapotis de leurs ailes alerte les hommes qui discutent
    autour de la table

les ventres blancs qui strient l'air méritent un bref salut
ce soir
avant de s'endormir
ils tourneront trois fois la clé dans la porte
cadenasseront leur coeur

***

Les vieilles de vieillesse s'inquiètent quand la lune n'est pas à
    sa place
se mirent dans leur mur quand elle surplombe leur toit sans
    s'arrêter

volaille serrée sous l'aisselle
elles tournent autour de leur cahute jusqu'à sa disparition
sourdes au vacarme des derniers rayons qui tombent dans un
    bruit de feuilles
alors que l'automne est passé de mode
devenu rumeur

***

The women who died in childbirth are reborn as feathered beasts
their down fills pillows
the flapping of their wings warns the men in heated
    discussion around a table

those white bellies streaking the air merit a hasty greeting
tonight
before going to sleep
they will turn the key three times in the door
padlock their hearts

***

The women ancient with age are uneasy when the moon is
    not in its place
gaze at their reflections in the wall when the moon rises
    above the roof without stopping

a hen tucked under their arm
they circle their shacks until it disappears
deaf to the din of the last rays that fall with a rustling of leaves
although autumn has gone out of fashion
become only a murmur

***

La femme qui troue l'eau de son bâton dégage un pays
    inférieur
l'enfant lové en lui-même rit de se voir si mort
elle l'appellerait si sa bouche n'était remplie d'abeilles

sa hache cachée sous sa jupe
elle tuera le bourdon
rendra son miel à la ruche
effacera d'un trait l'homme qui lape sa descendance entre ses
genoux

***

Visage de l'envieux fondu dans le plomb
c'est son oeil qui a émietté le feu comme noix de fin d'été
lui qui a soufflé la bougie du seuil

les gens de l'eau puisent leurs croyances dans le cheminement
    de l'ombre
là où les terres s'arrêtent

libre à vous d'y adhérer

***

The woman who pierces the water with her stick uncovers a
    lower country
the child curled up in himself laughs to see himself so dead
she would call to him if her mouth were not full of bees

with the axe hidden under her skirt
she will kill the bumblebee
bring the honey back to the hive
erase with one swipe the man who licks up his descendants
    between her knees

***

The envious man's face is melted in lead
it's his eye that crumbled up the fire like a walnut at the end of
    summer
he who blew out the candle on the threshold

the water people draw their beliefs from the shadow moving
    forward
there where the lands end

you're free to follow them

***

Les enfants entre deux terres dorment avec leur cerf-volant
affirment celles qui déplient du même geste leur linge et leurs
    champs

à l'enterrement du vent il n'y eut pas grand monde

les arbres devenus caduques
les oiseaux tombés des nids n'étaient pas assez mûrs
personne ne les ramassait
les gens avaient d'autres soucis

***

Celui qui revient après des années d'absence est un retourné
dans quel dialecte s'adressait-il aux loups qui mangeaient les
    traces de ses pas et se sentaient repus
a-t-il croisé l'ours la neige la fauvette
et à quel soleil cuisait-il son pain
a-t-il assez de bras pour arracher l'herbe qui a poussé sur son
    lit
assez d'yeux pour dormir
et un coeur à fendre à la hache lorsque les loups honteux de
    leur nudité
appellent l'homme vêtu de leur peau

***

The children between two lands sleep with their kites
say the women who unfold laundry and fields in one
    movement

not many came to the wind's funeral

the trees had become obsolete
and birds fallen from their nests weren't grown enough
no one picked them up
people had other problems

***

The man who comes back after years of absence is a revenant
in what dialect does he talk to the wolves who ate up his
    footsteps and felt full
did he cross the path of the bear the snow the hedge sparrow
and in what sun did he bake his bread
did he have enough arms to uproot all the grass that grew on
    his bed
enough eyes to sleep
and a heart to split with an axe when the wolves ashamed of
    their nudity
called to the man who was dressed in their skins

***

Un linge mouillé sur le front de l'arbre malade
les vieux de vieillesse invoquent les âmes périphériques et le
    dieu des abeilles
sauterelles ou criquets qu'importe quand pour d'obscures
    raisons les dernières ombres du jour dessinent un cercle
    infranchissable autour du tronc fiévreux
tisser un linceul assez vaste pour contenir les branches
    inséparables du vent devient urgent
même si la mort est suivie de guérison

***

Odeur de tourbe et de venaison sur les doigts de celui qui
    pleut l'amour en toute saison
son champ retourné avec sa herse
il retrace le même sillon rouge jusqu'à la femme qui fait son
    propre miel

qu'il soit homme ou orme
qu'il vienne d'un pli de la terre ou d'une strate de l'air
qu'il ait froissé l'orage ou mordu l'écorce
il est chez lui dans sa béance
dans ce tourbillon étourdissant de sucs et de chair retournée

***

A damp cloth on the sick tree's forehead
the men ancient with age call on the peripheral souls and the
   god of the bees
locusts or crickets what's the difference when for unknown
   reasons the last shadows of the day draw an impassable
   circle around the fevered trunk
it becomes urgent to weave a shroud vast enough to hold all
   the branches inseparable from the wind
even if death is followed by recovery

***

An odour of peat and venison on the fingers of the one who
   rains down love in all seasons
after he turned the soil with his harrow
he retraced the same furrow back to the woman who makes
   her own honey

whether he's a man or an elm tree
whether he comes from a furrow in the ground or a current
   of air
whether he offended the storm or bit into the bark
he is at home in the gape of her
in the deafening whirlpool of overturned sap and flesh

**

La forêt qui grignote du terrain finira dans le lit de la femme
    qui dort sur sa propre épaule
indécente sa robe rouge pour l'érable le seul à enjamber son
    seuil

à voix basses et pas de bousculade
interrompre le sommeil de l'endormie ferait sursauter ses
    volets clos sur un grand chagrin
la hache suspendue au mur ne coupe que l'air
parti avec le chemin celui qui mettait en déroute les branches
    belliqueuses qui faisaient le mur

**

Qu'ils s'empoignent ou s'étreignent
la forêt taiseuse fait celle qui n'a rien vu
seul le bûcheron peut faire la paix entre arbres belligérants
celui qui les a vus grandir n'a rien à se reprocher
donner sa ration de terre à la terre a raccourci ses bras et
    obscurci sa vue

la résine dit-il n'est ni semence ni sang mais sueur d'arbre
    récalcitrant

***

The forest that nibbles up fields will end up in the bed of the
    woman sleeping on her own shoulder
her red dress is indecent to the maple tree the only one who
    steps over her threshold

a low voice and no pushing or rushing
to interrupt her slumber would burst open her shutters
    locked on a great sorrow
the axe hung on the wall cuts down nothing but air
and the one who'd drive away the bellicose branches that leapt
    over the wall has gone with the road

***

Whether they fight or they kiss
the taciturn forest pretends to see nothing
only the woodcutter can make peace between warring trees
the one who watched them grow need blame himself for nothing
giving his share of earth to the earth has shortened his arms
    and darkened his vision

resin he says is neither sperm nor blood but the sweat of a
    recalcitrant tree

je suis d'un bois dont on fait les haches clame un chêne
    fatigué de vivre
mais personne ne le croit
car seuls les arbres morts quittent le monde de leur gré

***

Elle aurait voulu lui montrer le contenu de ses poches en
    chagrin et en cailloux
le persuader de s'allonger sur son herbe intime
branches croisées sur la poitrine dans l'attitude conforme à son état

jamais vu mort debout sur un seul pied
poussières agglutinées sous les ongles
aurait voulu lui dire que les flaques d'eau ne retiennent pas les
    gesticulations des arbres de passage
qu'elle l'aurait pleuré s'il était d'un bois moins inflammable
pleuré si elle savait pleurer

my wood is the kind that makes axe-handles, shouts an oak
    tired of living
but no one believes it
only dead trees leave this world of their own free will

***

She would have wanted to show him all the grief and pebbles
    in her pockets
persuade him to stretch out on her secret grasses
branches crossed on his chest as befit his condition

never saw a dead man standing on one foot
dust gathering under his fingernails
would have wanted to tell him that puddles don't retain the
    posturing of passing trees
that she would have wept if he were made of less flammable wood
wept if she knew how to weep

***

Lequel des deux pieds a la confiance du chemin
quel vent emporter dans la poche pour faire allégeance à la
    tempête
combien d'allumettes faut-il prévoir pour affronter l'éclair

celui qui porte sa maison sur son dos évite le bord du
    ravin
les pierres qui crient sous ses semelles ont la mémoire du
    premier caillou et la blessure du premier sillon
pierre et pain se mangeaient crus à l'époque
l'argile parlait
l'homme planté sur le sommet de la montagne attendait que
    la mer escalade la colline pour venir lécher ses orteils

***

Maison blanche percée d'une fenêtre noire
La femme qui creuse l'eau avec son bâton n'a pas su dessiner
    la porte

elle habite aux confins de l'écriture
ses mots pétris avec le même poids de farine et de frayeur

courir après la volaille a raccourci ses jambes et allongé son ruisseau

***

Which of your two feet does the road trust
what wind must you put in your pocket to swear the storm
    allegiance
how many matches are needed to brave the lightning

the one who carries his house on his back avoids the edge of
    the ravine
the stones that cry out beneath his soles have the first pebble's
    memories and the wound of the first furrow
stone and bread were eaten raw back then
the clay spoke
the man standing on the mountaintop was waiting for the sea
    to climb the hill and come lick his toes

***

White house with a black window set in it
The woman who dug for water with her stick didn't know
    how to draw the door

she lives at the borders of writing
her words are kneaded with equal parts flour and fear

chasing the chickens shortened her legs and lengthened her rivulet

aussi
quand le marc du café durcit dans sa tasse
elle qualifie la tourterelle grise de messager du malheur
la forêt d'armée d'envahisseurs
qui démantèleront ses mots et sa cahute
emporteront les murs
l'hiver pour seul interlocuteur
l'histoire n'en dit pas plus

***

Le vacarme des enfants qui jouent sous terre tarit le lait du
    figuier

pas de consolation à attendre de la photo
les corps endimanchés réduits à des traits
l'eau des visages a tourné au gel

comment expliquer ces pleurs lorsque la mère traîne le
    berceau jusqu'au fleuve frottant jusqu'à épuisement de
    ses forces le brou qui noircissait les petites mains qui
    continuent d'applaudir

also
when the coffee grounds harden in her cup
she calls the grey turtledove a messenger of misfortune
the forest an army of invaders
who dismantle her words and her hut
carry the walls away
with winter her one interlocutor
the story says no more about it

***

The racket the children make playing underground sours the
    fig tree's milk

no consolation will come from the photo
the bodies in their Sunday best pared down to lines
the faces' water turned to gel

how to explain the weeping when the mother drags the cradle
    as far as the river rubbing till she's exhausted the husk
    staining the little hands that keep on applauding

***

La femme d'eau douce s'accroche à son carré d'herbe pour
    résister aux nuages chapardeurs
sa bassine n'est pas assez profonde pour contenir ses frayeurs
sa fenêtre à ras de sol n'empêche pas ses enfants de s'envoler

inutile de demander l'aide du soleil qui rit d'un oeil et pleure
    de l'autre
ou l'intervention du vent qui se prend pour une foule depuis
    qu'il hurle dans tous les interstices
inutile de refaire les mêmes enfants avec la même argile s'ils
    ne savent pas pleurer

***

La femme qui saigne avec l'arbre ne remue pas son potage
ne connaît pas la teneur en tendresse de son oreiller ni la
    résistance de sa lanterne aux appels des passants
elle détruit sa masure toutes les nuits
la reconstruit le matin
face au figuier dont elle partage l'ombre et la peur
leur chair incandescente convoitée par ceux qui enjambent la clôture
mangent la peau jettent la pulpe derrière l'épaule
sourds à sa grande peine

***

The freshwater woman hangs on to her plot of grass to resist
    the thieving angels
her basin isn't deep enough to hold her fears
her window flush to the ground doesn't keep her children
    from flying away

useless to ask the sun for help, who laughs with one eye and
    weeps with the other
or for the wind's intervention, since it thinks it's a crowd since
    it howls in all the interstices
useless to make the same children out of the same clay if they
    don't know how to cry

***

The woman who bleeds with the tree doesn't stir her soup
doesn't know the tenderness content of her pillow nor her
    lantern's resistance to the cries of passersby
she tears down her hovel every night
and rebuilds it in the morning
facing the fig tree whose shade and fear she shares
those who climb over the fence lust after their incandescent flesh
eat the skin and throw the pulp over their shoulder
deaf to its pain

***

Comment savoir si les jeunes loups ont une mère
s'ils se cachent sous leur jupe par temps de désarroi et
        d'indigence
s'ils connaissent le chasseur qui rapièce les ailes déchiquetées
si sa femme le reçoit avec un jet de pierres lorsqu'il ramène
        une mère louve dans sa gibecière
et que faute de larmes elle fait pleurer le robinet

***

Que tu sois brouillard aux grandes enjambées ou homme
        chevillé à ses outils

tu coupes à la racine le blé noir de la femme malade
le brûles dans l'âtre avec les châtaignes

le bruit d'un flocon sur ton toit te précipite à l'extérieur
dos tourné à ta maison
tu fais don à l'hiver de ton champ
aux sauterelles de ta prochaine récolte
mais garde ta faucille pour tes vieux jours

souffler sur tes dix doigts ne réchauffe pas la neige qui se
        plaint du froid

***

Who knows if the young wolves have a mother
if they hide under her skirt in times of confusion and
    indigence
if they know the hunter who patches up torn wings
if his wife greets him with a volley of stones when he brings
    back a she-wolf in his game-bag
and if, for want of tears, she makes the tap weep

***

No matter if you're the wide-striding fog or the man pegged
    to his tools

you cut down the sick woman's black wheat at the root
and burn it on the hearth with the chestnuts

the sound of a snowflake on your roof sends you rushing outdoors
back turned to your house
you make a gift of your fields to winter
and your next harvest to the grasshoppers
but you keep your scythe for your old age

blowing on your ten fingers doesn't warm the snow when it
    complains about the cold

***

Un temps à ne pas laisser un chemin dehors
tu essores sa pluie
le sèches sur ta corde
lui prêtes ta couverture en poil de chèvre
mais te fâches lorsqu'il te suit à l'intérieur
un affront à ton linge la boue sur ses semelles
sa buée offense à ton miroir

qu'a-t-il dit de si triste pour que les cailloux de ton jardin se
    mettent à pleurer

***

Regarder le nuage dans le blanc des yeux fait larmoyer tes
    vitres
trop courte ton échelle pour reculer l'hiver d'un hiver

tu ne balaies plus devant ta porte
ne donnes plus à manger à ton mort familier

l'homme à la gibecière t'avait promis une maison à l'intérieur
    de ta maison
un seuil en pierres blanches
et une fenêtre ouverte sur les cinq continents

***

You wouldn't leave a road outdoors on a night like this
you wring out its tears
hang it on the line to dry
lend it your goatskin blanket
but you get angry when it follows you inside
its muddy soles an insult to your clean linens
its mist an offense to your mirror

what did it say that was so sad the pebbles in your garden
    started to cry?

***

Staring straight into the cloud's eyes makes your
    windowpanes whimper
your ladder is too short to push the winter one winter back

you no longer sweep in front of your door
or give your household's dead man anything to eat

the man with the game-bag had promised you a house inside
    the house
a doorstep made of white stones
and a window open on the five continents

son ombre allongée sur ton lit
il entend tes ahanements lorsque tu charges la porte sur ton
dos pour la protéger des voleurs
et que personne n'est là pour témoigner

***

Les murs ne l'ont pas retenue lorsqu'elle lança par la fenêtre
les miettes et les enfants
jetés pour qu'ils n'aient plus peur du loup
pour ne pas vieillir avec l'herbe
mourir avec le figuier

posés sur le même espace
loup femme figuier n'ont pas la même perception du temps
la femme éteint sa lampe quand le loup se réveille
l'arbre insomniaque surveille leurs déplacements
les trois deviennent deux par temps de neige et de suspicion
quand le figuier et les cheveux de la femme blanchissent
d'un coup et que le loup qui ne les reconnaît plus se sent
si seul

his shadow stretched out on your bed
he hears your panting when you carry the door on your back
    to protect it from thieves
with no one there to bear witness

***

The walls didn't stop her when she hurled
crumbs and children out the window
threw them so they wouldn't be afraid of the wolf
wouldn't grow old with the grass
die with the fig tree

placed in the same space
wolf woman fig tree don't have the same perception of time
the woman puts out her lamp when the wolf wakes up
the insomniac tree observes their displacements
the three become two in seasons of snow and suspicion
    when the fig tree and the woman's hair turn white all at
    once and the wolf who doesn't recognize them feels so
    lonely

***

Désarroi de l'homme qui a troqué son livre contre une maison
les murs effeuillés ne recèlent aucun message
ne racontent pas la douleur de celui qui l'a bâtie
les empoignades entre vents rivaux sous sa fenêtre
incapable de déchiffrer leurs hurlements

***

Elle goûte l'eau bouillante de la lessive pour évaluer la
    résistance du linge à la douleur
manque et plénitude constituent ses journées
manque du coq emporté par le renard et celle de l'homme qui
    tua le renard puis disparut dans son terrier
sa chaussure égarée sur le chemin le ramènera à sa vie se dit-
    elle quand un bruit de semelles écrase les cailloux
quand l'ombre de chaque arbre devient un visiteur

Confusion of the man who bartered his book for a house
leaf through the walls but they hide no message
don't tell of the sorrow of the one who built it
the arguments of rival winds beneath his window
and he can't decipher their howling

She tastes the boiling washing water to judge the laundry's
    resistance to pain
her days are made of lack and plenitude
lack of the rooster the fox carried off and of the man who
    killed the fox and then disappeared in its den
the shoe he lost on the path will bring him back to his life she says
    to herself when there's the sound of soles crushing pebbles
when the shadow of each tree becomes a visitor

Afterword

Reading Vénus Khoury-Ghata's *The Water People* is to luxuriate in the sun, in a hammock, on a sultry afternoon; it is to enter a dream-state that opens onto a strange, yet familiar world, where humanity is at one with its environment, where an animist communication with other life forms – trees, stones, rivers – is possible, quotidian even.

Perhaps this place is situated in an ancient, Edenic, pre-apocalyptic era, where the ravages of the extractive, industrial complex have yet to make their wounding mark; perhaps the water people are post-flood survivors; or perhaps it is a contigious locale, a world adjacent to that which we currently 'occupy', where humanity's decisions follow an alternative fork in the path, and our communal interactions with the planet, as 'a people', have been integrated, and kindly.

Whichever reality we choose to alight on, and it might be one or a combination of many, what we can draw from this selection from Khoury-Ghata's lush book-length poem is an invitation to consider 'nature' poetry in a new way for the 21st century. In this sense, we can think of *The Water People* as ecological poetry, as verse that impels us to listen to the messages brought to us from the meta-human world with urgent attention. Like Louise Glück's *The Wild Iris*, it is a ventriloquist work that encourages an ecocritical reading through which we might grapple with the many paradoxical complexities that modernity presents. Here, though, modernity is most present in its absence: the book's vocabulary is one of the 'she-wolf', the 'scythe', the 'lantern' and the 'hunter', nouns that populate a landscape where 'only the woodcutter can make peace between warring trees'. These archetypal words and phrases collectively evoke the fairy tale and the creation myth, before such allegories were cleansed of the surreal and the macabre in favour of a more sanitised narrative deemed suitable for children and young adults by Hollywood and its ilk.

As one might expect from a cosmos populated by water people, the poems here are fluid, the language supple and mellifluous. Yet there is insistence in the communication, an insistence that is amplified by anaphora and refrain. The book opens with an imperative: 'Weep as if the river had entered you', the speaker commands, 'And leave your voice behind to listen better when it rains.' The water people, we learn, have mouths that are 'full of bees'; while bees make honey, they also sting.

A yearling kid is 'dismembered bare-handed', while the 'woman of the water people' is so powerful and violent that she:

makes death submit
go down on its knees.

The relationship with violence is resonant and disturbing. It also provokes us to interrogate our own reading of the text and what we elicit from it. Should we be glad that death gives in, or do we end up pitying death? Is death a political prisoner, the victim rather than the aggressor? Are we witnessing a vicious circle, trapped in a cycle of retribution?

Another unnamed woman who has an 'axe hidden under her skirt' will 'kill the bumblebee' and 'bring the honey back to the hive'. We know that ecologically bees are imperilled, but Khoury-Ghata extends the danger nature faces to larger elemental entities, stating that 'not many came to the wind's funeral'. This is how we learn that the wind is dead. The post-apocalyptic possibilities are imminent, as the absence of wind suggests a world in which the fundamental elements no longer exist. When fledglings fall from their nests no-one picks them up because 'people had other problems'. It is a cool accounting and as nature collapses human life goes on, if not blithely then defiantly. Despite the fact that the signs are there before us, obvious and extreme, humans are unable to heed the warnings, our fate has already been determined, the consequences of our indifference are inescapable.

Elsewhere the tone is declarative, a condition of world- and myth-making and a strategy which again brings with it the ring of fable or folklore. The villagers that gather around the fire and its embers are both wise and innocent, and they come to us in the plural, as earthly beings, who inhabit a paradise that if not lost is shrouded by beings who manifest as a 'benevolent fog'.

Trees are ubiquitous and anthropomorphic characters that merge with a societal womanhood. So we encounter the girl who 'uproots a stream from the earth to wash off the pomegranate tree's menstrual blood' and the mother who teaches the pubescent girl 'to shave the female trees' armpits'. In the pomegranate we are immediately reminded of Persephone, and with her the fruit's symbolic representations of sexuality, death and fecundity that endure in European and Arab literatures. There is also an 'empathy tree', but, the speaker warns, asking its advice is 'only good for the dead'. This admonishment strikes a stark note, reminding us of humanity's fickle and exploitative shortcomings, as well as the frustrating realities of hindsight.

If, as W H Auden declared in his poem sequence 'Bucolics', 'A culture is no better than its woods', then we might read Khoury-Ghata's forested dreamscape as a place to enter with caution. 'My wood is the kind that makes axe-handles' is the cry of a suicidal oak who is dismissed because 'only dead trees leave this world of their own free will.' We also learn that the water people take their 'codes' from the willow, bury those they have killed at the foot of the yew, and a 'taciturn' forest comprised of 'bellicose branches' 'nibbles up fields', a phrase that spotlights the competition between wilderness and agriculture. Nonetheless, even though the water people's world is imperilled, it is a world with trees surviving (if not always thriving) in it.

Whilst the divisions between energetic entities and humans are porous, the lines between men and women are distinct and, if we are so minded, can be read as a feminist critique of war and violence. 'Armed with his anger/the man hunts to hear his explosions pierce the sky/to make it rain and quench his corn stalks' thirst' is one of many aphoristic phrases that populate *The Water People*, as is the metaphorically alluring 'The man who pierced the cloud with his slingshot will have only a puddle to weep for him'.

Despite these patriarchal overtones, the women of the water people are not submissive or cowed: they 'feed the tiger with their bare hands', and 'are 'entitled to one rooster but to three men'.

For want of a mirror
the women of the water people don't know that they are
women

And yet they do. Women in labour wear bracelets that jangle, the local shamaness (who is not, notably, a witch) prescribes a charm for the harvest, the repetition of the word 'harrow', which both evokes our relationship with the soil, the field, and also reminds us that life can be harrowing.

The poems are peppered with aphorisms that are recognisable not only through their content and idiom but also through a song-like quality which is a trademark of Khoury-Ghata's intensely lyric voice. This in turn refers us to the ghazal, where each couplet is a self-contained entity, where the cry of the gazelle is one of poignancy, if not mourning.

We are also reminded of the riddle, where each statement is a leaf that unfurls as part of a larger puzzle, a puzzle that reveals its meaning via a prismatic structure that resists easy interpretation or linear logic.

Khoury-Ghata is an expatriate of her native Lebanon and in many senses these are poems which celebrate the liminality of 'othered' space whilst still acknowledging the frustration of exile. As she puts it, the woman who 'tears down her hovel every night' is one who 'rebuilds it in the morning'. If war is inevitable, or an eternal human condition, then our capacity for resilience and resistance is equally enduring, albeit exhausting. This is her great skill, to deftly encompass the abyss between moments of huge and often catastrophic contrast, to straddle moments of light and dark with elegance and ease.

The Water People is a collection which bears multiple re-readings, with each occasion offering a new transformative rendition that may be similar yet different to the last. The poet urges us to embrace these moments of paradox and complexity to acknowledge that we are no more (and possibly less) wise than the flora and fauna with whom we share our home. If we mourn we must do so with mirth. Nothing is black or white, rather it is black and white, and in Khoury-Ghata's universe, even the mighty sun 'laughs with one eye and weeps with the other'.

Karen McCarthy Woolf

Lebanese poet and novelist, long-time Paris resident Vénus Khoury-Ghata is the author of 23 novels including *Une Maison aux bord des larmes* (translated by Marilyn Hacker as *A House at the Edge of Tears*, Graywolf Press, 2005) and *La Femme qui ne savait pas garder les hommes*; *Les Derniers Jours de Mandelstam*, an imaginative biography; and 21 collections of poems, including *Eloignez-vous de ma fenêtre* (Mercure de France, 2021) and *Gens de l'eau* (Mercure de France, 2018), from which the poems in this World Poetry Series book are taken. Other collections of Khoury-Ghata's poems available in English in Marilyn Hacker's translation include *Alphabets of Sand* (Carcanet Press, 2009), *Where are the trees going?* (Northwestern University Press, 2014) and *A Handful of Blue Earth* (Liverpool University Press, 2017). Recipient of the Académie Française prize for poetry in 2009, Khoury-Ghata was named an Officer of the Légion d'honneur the following year. She received the Prix Goncourt de poésie in 2011.

Marilyn Hacker is the author of fourteen books of poems, including *A Stranger's Mirror* (Norton, 2015) and *Blazons* (Carcanet, 2019); an essay collection, *Unauthorized Voices* (Michigan, 2010); and eighteen collections of translations of French and Francophone poets also including Samira Negrouche, Jean-Paul de Dadelsen and Claire Malroux. *A Different Distance*, a collaborative sequence written with Karthika Naïr, was published by Milkweed Editions in 2021. Her awards include the National Book Award, the 2009 American PEN award for poetry in translation and the 2010 PEN Voelcker Award. She lives in Paris.

Born in London to English and Jamaican parents, Karen McCarthy Woolf is a Fulbright postdoctoral scholar, the author of two poetry collections and the editor of six literary anthologies. Shortlisted for the Forward, Felix Dennis and Jerwood Prizes, her début *An Aviary of Small Birds* tells the story of losing a son in childbirth and was an *Observer* Book of the Year. Her latest, *Seasonal Disturbances*, explores gentrification, the city and the sacred, and was a winner in the inaugural Laurel Prize for Ecological Poetry.

About the Poetry Translation Centre

Set up in 2004, the Poetry Translation Centre is the only UK organisation dedicated to translating, publishing and promoting contemporary poetry from Africa, Asia, the Middle East and Latin America. We introduce extraordinary poets from around the world to new audiences through books, online resources and bilingual events. We champion diversity and representation in the arts and forge enduring relations with diaspora communities in the UK. We explore the craft of translation through our long-running programme of workshops which are open to all.

The Poetry Translation Centre is based in London and is an Arts Council National Portfolio organisation. To find out more about us, including how you can support our work, please visit: www.poetrytranslation.org.

About the World Poet Series

The *World Poet Series* offers an introduction to some of the world's most exciting contemporary poets in an elegant pocket-sized format. The books are presented as bilingual editions, with the English and original-language text displayed side by side. They include specially commissioned translations and completing each book is an afterword essay by a UK-based poet, responding to the translations.